Emmett Sees You

Written by Kate Nicoll

*To all the children, including my own,
who brought back my sense of wonder.*

*With gratitude to my dear husband, Karl,
for supporting my dream of Soul Friends.*

*Any day spent with you is my favorite day.
So today is my favorite day.*

– A.A. Milne, Winnie the Pooh

Emmett sees you.
He sees your beautiful eyes...

He wonders what do you
see?

Trees? The sky? Stars?
Tell him, what you see?

Emmett sees your kindness
He sees it in your smile...

He is curious when did you smile today?
Tell him, what made you glow?

Emmett sees your sense of wonder...

He sees it in watching your
brain working
and
wheels turning...

He is wondering what
curious thoughts you had today.

Tell him,
what you were wondering?

Emmett sees you are caring.
He sees it in your reaching out your hand to
help or hold…

He is curious how you shared today.
Tell him what you did in giving to others?

Emmett sees your
feelings in your heart.

He sees it in how you show
caring with others...

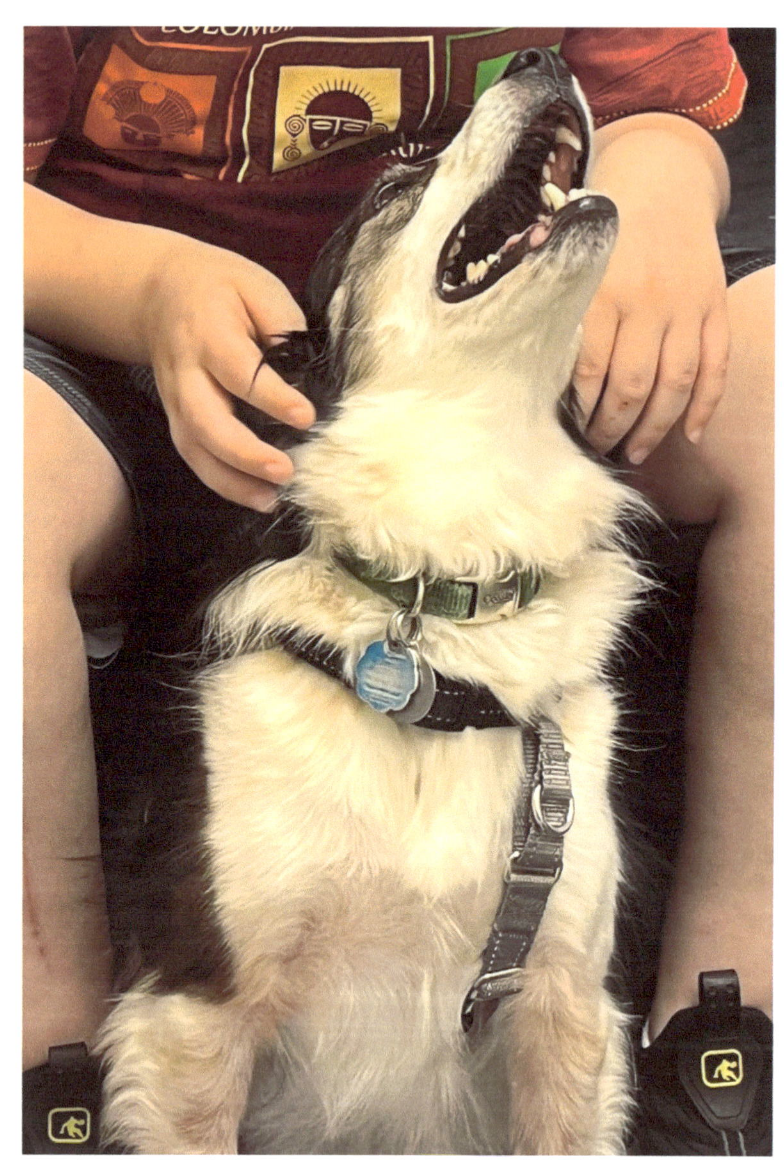

He wonders who you shared your feelings with.
Tell him about your feelings today
and who listened?

Emmett sees your delight
He sees a sparkle in you, a strength within you...

He is curious how you felt a sparkle within you today
Tell him what makes you, wonderful you!

"By presenting queries from the point of view of a dog, Kate Nicoll uses children's natural kinship with companion animals to take them on a guided journey to a more grounded and prosocial relation to self and others.

In this simple but powerful instrument, children are sensitized to sight and touch and, through them, to a sense of wonder and caring."

Kenneth Shapiro, PhD
President, Board of Directors
Animals & Society Institute

"This book helps you see yourself for who you are."

Brooke, Age 10

Kate Nicoll is a graduate of Elms College and Smith College, with several post-master certifications in the healing benefits of the human-animal bond.

Kate is also the Founder of Soul Friends, a non profit who provides innovative clinical and educational programs that promote the healing benefits of the human-animal bond and nature for children, families, young adults, veterans and first responders.

To learn more about Kate and her work with animal assisted therapy, please visit www.soul-friends.org

Healing the hearts of children and families one wagging tail at a time